COUP D'ÉTAT IN AFRICA

MILITARY TAKEOVER AND POLITICAL TURMOIL IN AFRICA

NICOLE GODFREY.

CONTENTS:

STRENGTHENING DEMOCRACY

IMPROVING GOVERNANCE

FIGHTING CORRUPTION

PROMOTING ECONOMIC DEVELOPMENT

REFORMING THE MILITARY

ENSURING CIVILIAN CONTROL OF THE
MILITARY

PROVIDING BETTER TRAINING AND
EDUCATION FOR SOLDIERS

INTRODUCTION

In the annals of modern African history, the specter of coups d'état has cast a long and turbulent shadow over the continent's political landscape. The African continent, a vast mosaic of cultures, nations, and peoples, has, regrettably, witnessed numerous coups that have shaped its political destiny. This intricate tapestry of power struggles, coups, and counter-coups has left an indelible mark on the socio-political development of the region.

We delve into the historical context of coups d'état in Africa, elucidating their causes, consequences, and key examples of such events in Mali, Niger, Gabon, and Côte d'Ivoire. To truly understand the intricate web of coups on this vast continent, one must venture deep into the historical roots that have incubated these crises, exploring the multifaceted factors that have fueled this tumultuous chapter in Africa's history.

BACKGROUND OF THE COUP D'ÉTAT IN AFRICA

The emergence of coups d'état as a recurrent phenomenon in Africa is inextricably linked to the continent's complex colonial legacy. Africa, the cradle of ancient civilizations, was subjected to a prolonged period of European colonization, which persisted well into the 20th century. The aftermath of decolonization saw the emergence of numerous newly independent nations, struggling to establish stable governance structures.

Colonial rule often left a fragmented political landscape, with arbitrary borders imposed by colonial powers. These borders seldom respected the ethnic, cultural, and religious realities on the ground, fostering conditions ripe for political unrest. As post-colonial nations grappled with the daunting task of nation-building, the absence of a strong institutional foundation and the legacy of divisive colonial policies became breeding grounds for political instability.

One hallmark of African coups has been the prominence of military intervention in politics. In the absence of well-established civilian institutions, African militaries often became pivotal actors in shaping the destiny of their nations. This military involvement in politics has led to a recurring pattern of coup d'état as a means of acquiring and consolidating power.

Furthermore, economic factors have played a substantial role in fomenting political unrest. Africa's vast natural resources, while a source of potential wealth, have too often been a curse. The struggle for control over these resources has frequently been a trigger for political upheaval, as elites and foreign interests vied for dominance.

Coups in Mali, Niger, Gabon, and Côte d'Ivoire

1. Mali

Mali, a nation situated in the heart of West Africa, has experienced its fair share of coups. One of the most notable was the March 2012 coup led by Captain Amadou Haya Sanogo, which ousted President Amadou Toumani Touré. The coup was motivated by allegations of corruption, mismanagement, and the government's perceived inability to address the Tuareg rebellion in the north.

Mali's coup was emblematic of the complex interplay between political instability, ethnic tensions, and the military's role in African politics. The repercussions of this coup reverberated across the region, culminating in a French-led military intervention to combat Islamist militants in northern Mali.

2. Niger

Niger, a landlocked nation in the Sahel region, has grappled with political instability and a series of coups since its independence from France in 1960. In February 2010, President Mamadou Tandja was overthrown in a coup led by Salou Djibo. This coup was driven by Tandja's controversial bid to extend his presidency and concentrate power.

Niger's coups have often been intertwined with issues of constitutional manipulation and political power struggles. The nation's vast mineral wealth, particularly uranium, has also attracted international interests and contributed to its political volatility.

3. Gabon

Gabon, located in Central Africa, is another country that has experienced coups. In 1967, a military coup led by Jean-Hilaire Aubame and Omar Bongo ousted President Léon M'ba. Omar Bongo subsequently consolidated power and ruled Gabon for more than four decades until his death in 2009.

Gabon's coups have been characterized by the concentration of power within a single political family and a lack of political pluralism. The nation's oil wealth has played a significant role in sustaining this authoritarian rule.

4. Côte d'Ivoire

Côte d'Ivoire, in West Africa, has a tumultuous history of political instability and coups. One of the most notable coups occurred in 1999 when General Robert Guéï seized power from President Henri Konan Bédié. This coup was rooted in economic grievances, political exclusion, and ethnic tensions.

Côte d'Ivoire's coups have often been marked by deep-seated political and ethnic divisions, exacerbated by competition for cocoa and coffee exports, which are crucial to the nation's economy.

The prevalence of coups d'état in Africa is deeply intertwined with a complex web of historical, political, economic, and social factors. The examples of Mali, Niger, Gabon, and Côte d'Ivoire offer a glimpse into the diverse dynamics that have fueled these political upheavals. Understanding these factors is crucial for envisioning a more stable and prosperous future for the African continent, where democratic governance and the rule of law can flourish, ultimately providing the foundation for sustainable development and peace.

There are a number of factors that contribute to coups in Africa. Some of the most common causes include:

Political instability: Many African countries are characterized by political instability, which can make them vulnerable to coups. This instability can be caused by a number of factors, such as ethnic conflict, religious tensions, or economic problems.

Economic problems: Economic problems can also lead to coups. When people are struggling to make ends meet, they may be more likely to support a coup that promises to bring about change.

Military intervention: The military can also play a role in coups. In some cases, the military may intervene to overthrow a government that it sees as corrupt or incompetent.

Foreign interference: Foreign powers have sometimes been involved in coups in Africa. This can be done through providing financial or logistical support to coup plotters, or by providing political cover for a coup.

CHAPTER 1

A Historical Overview of Coups in African Countries

The history of coups in African countries is a tale of political upheaval, power struggles, and societal change. This continent, with its diverse cultures, languages, and histories, has witnessed numerous coups over the decades, each with its unique context and consequences. To truly understand the dynamics and impact of coups in Africa, it's essential to embark on a historical journey that unravels this complex tapestry.

Early Coups and Colonial Legacy

The roots of coups in Africa can be traced back to the colonial era when European powers established their dominion over the continent. Many African nations experienced significant political and social upheaval during colonization, and this period laid the foundation for future coups.

In the immediate post-colonial period, coups were relatively rare, but the legacy of colonialism left a deep imprint on African nations. Newly independent countries often grappled with fragile institutions, ethnic divisions, and a lack of experience in democratic governance.

The 1960s and 1970s: The Era of Coups

The 1960s and 1970s marked a tumultuous period in African history, characterized by a surge in coup d'états. Numerous African nations, including Ghana, Nigeria, the Democratic Republic of Congo, and Mali, experienced coups during this era.

Many of these coups were driven by a desire to remove corrupt or authoritarian leaders, address perceived economic injustices, or combat ethnic and regional tensions. Military officers, often disillusioned with the post-colonial political elite, played a prominent role in these coups.

The Cold War and Superpower Influence

During the Cold War, Africa became a battleground for superpower influence. The United States and the Soviet Union often supported opposing factions in African nations, exacerbating political instability and contributing to the occurrence of coups.

Superpower rivalry led to proxy wars, arms proliferation, and the use of African nations as pawns in the global struggle for supremacy. This geopolitical context further fueled the propensity for coups in the region.

Authoritarianism and One-Party Rule

Many African countries experienced prolonged periods of authoritarian rule and one-party systems in the decades following independence. Leaders clung to power, often through rigged elections and suppression of political opposition. The frustration and discontent stemming from these repressive regimes created fertile ground for coup attempts.

In some cases, coups were framed as efforts to restore democratic governance or eliminate dictatorial leaders. However, coups themselves often led to military regimes that perpetuated authoritarianism.

Regional Variation

The history of coups in African countries is not uniform; it varies widely from one region to another. North Africa, for example, saw several military interventions during the Arab Spring in

2011, while West Africa has witnessed a history of frequent coups.

Southern Africa, on the other hand, has had relatively fewer coups, partly due to the prevalence of liberation movements-turned-governing parties in the post-independence period. East Africa has experienced a mix of coup attempts and authoritarian rule, with countries like Ethiopia and Sudan undergoing significant political changes.

Challenges to Democracy

While there have been significant strides toward democracy in Africa since the early 1990s, coups continue to pose challenges to democratic governance. In some cases, leaders who came to power through coups have managed to legitimize their rule through elections, blurring the lines between authoritarianism and democracy.

Elections, while a positive step, have sometimes been marred by irregularities, allegations of fraud, and disputes, leading to further political instability and, occasionally, coup attempts.

Recent Trends and Responses

In recent years, there has been a notable resurgence of coups in Africa. Nations like Sudan and Mali have experienced coups driven by grievances over corruption, economic mismanagement, and perceived lack of political reform.

The international community, regional organizations, and African nations themselves have responded to these coups with a mix of diplomatic pressure, sanctions, and calls for the restoration of constitutional order. The African Union (AU) and regional economic communities have played critical roles in mediating conflicts and seeking peaceful solutions.

Major coups in Africa

Major coups in Africa, including the recent ones in various countries in Africa

1960s: The 1960s was a decade of political instability in Africa, with many countries experiencing coups. Some of the most notable coups of the 1960s include:

The 1966 coup in Ghana, which overthrew Kwame Nkrumah, the first president of Ghana.

The 1969 coup in Nigeria, which overthrew General Yakubu Gowon, the head of state of Nigeria.

The 1971 coup in Uganda, which overthrew Milton Obote, the president of Uganda.

1970s: The 1970s saw a continuation of the coup trend in Africa. Some of the most notable coups of the 1970s include:

The 1972 coup in Somalia, which overthrew Mohamed Siad Barre, the president of Somalia.

The 1975 coup in Angola, which overthrew the Popular Movement for the Liberation of Angola (MPLA).

The 1979 coup in Liberia, which overthrew William R. Tolbert, Jr., the president of Liberia.

1980s: The 1980s saw a decline in the number of coups in Africa. However, there were still some notable coups, such as:

The 1983 coup in Burkina Faso, which overthrew Thomas Sankara, the president of Burkina Faso.

The 1987 coup in Ethiopia, which overthrew Mengistu Haile Mariam, the president of Ethiopia.

The 1989 coup in Sudan, which overthrew Gaafar Nimeiry, the president of Sudan.

1990s: The 1990s saw a further decline in the number of coups in Africa. This was due to a number of factors, including the end of the Cold War and the spread of democracy in Africa. However, there were still some notable coups, such as:

The 1991 coup in Sierra Leone, which overthrew Joseph Saidu Momoh, the president of Sierra Leone.

The 1992 coup in Niger, which overthrew Mahamane Ousmane, the president of Niger.

The 1997 coup in Sierra Leone, which overthrew Ahmad Tejan Kabbah, the president of Sierra Leone.

2000s: The 2000s saw a resurgence of coups in Africa. Some of the most notable coups of the 2000s include:

The 2002 coup in Guinea-Bissau, which overthrew Kumba Ialá, the president of Guinea-Bissau.

The 2003 coup in the Central African Republic, which overthrew Ange-Félix Patassé, the president of the Central African Republic.

The 2009 coup in Mauritania, which overthrew Sidi Ould Cheikh Abdallahi, the president of Mauritania.

2010s: The 2010s saw a continuation of the coup trend in Africa. Some of the most notable coups of the 2010s include:

The 2012 coup in Mali, which overthrew Amadou Toumani Touré, the president of Mali.

The 2013 coup in Guinea-Bissau, which overthrew Raimundo Pereira, the president of Guinea-Bissau.

The 2015 coup in Burkina Faso, which overthrew Michel Kafando, the interim president of Burkina Faso.

2020s: The 2020s have seen a number of coups in Africa, including:

The 2020 coup in Mali, which overthrew Ibrahim Boubacar Keïta, the president of Mali.

The 2021 coup in Chad, which overthrew Idriss Déby, the president of Chad.

The 2021 coup in Guinea, which overthrew Alpha Condé, the president of Guinea.

The 2022 coup in Burkina Faso, which overthrew Roch Marc Christian Kaboré, the president of Burkina Faso.

2023 Nigerien coup d'état: On July 26, 2023, the presidential guard of the Republic of the Niger detained President Mohamed Bazoum.

CHAPTER 2

Causes of the Coup d'État in Africa

Africa's turbulent history has been punctuated by a recurring phenomenon that has left an indelible mark on its political landscape: the coup d'état. These abrupt seizures of power have, time and again, disrupted the continent's socio-political trajectory, hindering its developmental aspirations. To comprehensively examine the root causes of coups d'état in Africa, it is imperative to scrutinize the intricate interplay of political instability, economic woes, military intervention, foreign interference, and other complex factors that have contributed to this enduring crisis.

Political Instability

Political instability has been a perennial challenge for many African nations. It often stems from a confluence of factors, including weak democratic institutions, power struggles, and a lack of political inclusivity. In the absence of strong and inclusive governance structures, power becomes concentrated, creating fertile ground for dissent and coup attempts.

Leadership transitions, especially those marred by contested elections or the manipulation of constitutional term limits, have been catalysts for coups. When leaders cling to power beyond their mandates, disenchantment among the populace grows, leading to an environment ripe for military intervention.

Moreover, ethnic and regional divisions can exacerbate political instability. In many African countries, ethnic loyalties often take precedence over national identities, making it challenging to build a cohesive and inclusive political system. Political actors exploit these divisions, further fragmenting societies and fostering an environment conducive to coups.

Economic Problems

Economic factors play a pivotal role in the genesis of coups d'état in Africa. High levels of poverty, unemployment, and economic inequality create discontent and frustration among the populace. When governments fail to address these economic challenges, it can trigger public unrest and provide an impetus for military intervention.

Resource-dependent economies are particularly vulnerable to coups. The mismanagement or exploitation of valuable resources, such as oil, diamonds, or minerals, can be a driving force behind coup attempts. The competition for control over these resources often involves powerful elites and foreign interests, intensifying political turmoil.

Economic crises, whether induced by corruption, mismanagement, or external shocks, can also serve as a tipping point for coups. When governments are unable to provide basic services, maintain price stability, or ensure economic growth, discontent swells, making it easier for military factions to garner support for a coup.

Military Intervention

Perhaps one of the most defining features of coups in Africa is the prominent role played by the military. Historically, African militaries have often been the arbiters of political power. The military's involvement in politics can be traced back to the colonial legacy, where armed forces were established primarily to maintain colonial rule.

Weak civilian institutions, coupled with a lack of civilian control over the military, have enabled military leaders to exploit power vacuums for their own gain. In some cases, military officers who perceive political leaders as corrupt or inept may justify coups as a means to rescue the nation from perceived misrule.

Furthermore, military intervention is facilitated by the availability of weapons and training. The proliferation of arms and military aid from foreign powers has often empowered military factions to stage coups with relative ease.

Foreign Interference

Foreign interference has been a recurring theme in African coups. External actors, including foreign governments and multinational corporations, often meddle in the affairs of African nations to protect their interests or advance their geopolitical agendas.

Foreign support can manifest in various ways, including financial backing for coup plotters, covert intelligence operations, or even direct military intervention. The presence of foreign military bases on African soil has, at times, fueled resentment and acted as a catalyst for coup attempts.

Furthermore, the manipulation of African leaders by foreign powers can create political instability. Leaders who align themselves with external actors may face opposition from domestic factions that perceive them as puppets of foreign interests, potentially leading to coup attempts.

Ethnic and Religious Tensions

Ethnic and religious tensions are potent drivers of political instability and coup attempts in Africa. Many African nations are ethnically diverse, with complex webs of intergroup relationships. When these tensions are exploited by political actors for personal gain, it can lead to violence and insecurity.

Religious divisions, often exacerbated by external factors such as the global spread of extremist ideologies, have also contributed to instability. In some cases, religious tensions have intersected with political disputes, creating a volatile mix that can precipitate coups.

Additional causes that contribute to the occurrence of coups d'état in Africa:

Corruption and Mismanagement

Corruption and mismanagement of state resources have been pervasive problems in many African nations. When political leaders and elites siphon off public funds for personal enrichment, it not only deprives the population of essential services but also fuels widespread anger and discontent. This discontent can coalesce into support for coup attempts, with the promise of ending corruption often being a central rallying cry for coup plotters.

Youth Unemployment and Disenfranchisement

Africa has a disproportionately youthful population, and high levels of youth unemployment can be a volatile cocktail for political instability. Young people, who make up a significant portion of the population, often feel disenfranchised when they are excluded from economic and political opportunities. This frustration can find an outlet in supporting or participating in coup attempts, especially when they perceive that existing political elites are not addressing their concerns.

Civil Conflicts and Insurgencies

Countries facing ongoing civil conflicts or insurgencies are particularly susceptible to coups. Armed rebel groups often operate in regions with weak government control, and their activities can destabilize the country as a whole. Military factions may justify coups as necessary to restore order or combat insurgent threats. The complex relationships between rebel groups, the military, and political leaders can create a chaotic environment ripe for coups.

Legacy of Authoritarian Rule

Many African nations have experienced a legacy of authoritarian rule, where leaders wielded unchecked power for extended periods. This legacy can contribute to a culture of political repression and intolerance of dissent. When attempts are made to transition to democracy, entrenched elites may resist, leading to political crises and coup attempts as a means of preserving their dominance.

External Debt and Economic Dependence

African countries burdened by high levels of external debt and economic dependence on foreign aid or loans can find themselves in precarious situations. The conditions imposed by international financial institutions may include austerity measures that are deeply unpopular among the population. When governments acquiesce to these demands, they risk losing public support and may face coup attempts from within the military or disgruntled factions.

Weak Rule of Law and Judicial Independence

The absence of a robust and independent judiciary can undermine the rule of law, making it easier for leaders to manipulate legal processes to their advantage. This can lead to political impunity, where leaders engage in illegal activities without consequence. When citizens perceive that there is no avenue for legal recourse, they may turn to military intervention as a last resort to address grievances.

Historical Grievances and Ethnic Divisions

Historical grievances, such as unresolved conflicts or land disputes, can simmer beneath the surface for years, contributing to political instability. Ethnic divisions and tensions may be exploited by political actors to mobilize support or foment unrest. Coups can be seen as a means of addressing these historical grievances, whether real or perceived, and can quickly escalate into larger conflicts.

Media Suppression and Censorship

In some African nations, the media is tightly controlled or subject to censorship. When information is restricted and citizens are denied access to unbiased reporting, it can create a climate of misinformation and propaganda. In such environments, rumors and conspiracy theories can gain traction, further destabilizing the political landscape and potentially leading to coup attempts as a response to perceived threats.

The causes of coups d'état in Africa are multifaceted and interconnected. Political instability, economic problems, military intervention, foreign interference, corruption, youth disenfranchisement, civil conflicts, and historical grievances all contribute to the occurrence of coups.

Addressing these complex challenges requires comprehensive strategies that encompass political, economic, and social reforms, as well as measures to strengthen democratic institutions and promote good governance. Additionally, international cooperation and support for African nations in their efforts to address these issues are crucial in reducing the frequency and impact of coups in the region.

The causes of coups d'état in Africa are multifaceted, reflecting a complex interplay of political, economic, military, and foreign factors. Addressing these root causes requires a holistic approach that encompasses building strong democratic institutions, promoting economic development, ensuring civilian control over the military, and curbing foreign interference.

African nations must strive for political inclusivity, transparent governance, and the equitable distribution of resources to mitigate the conditions that foster coups. International cooperation should focus on supporting democratic governance, conflict prevention, and the responsible management of Africa's abundant natural resources.

In this endeavor, it is essential to recognize that the solutions to the coup epidemic in Africa must be tailored to each nation's unique circumstances. A one-size-fits-all approach is unlikely to succeed in addressing the intricate web of challenges that underpin coup attempts on the continent. Only through concerted efforts at both the national and international levels can Africa hope to break free from the cycle of coups and chart a more stable and prosperous future.

CHAPTER 3

CONSEQUENCES OF THE COUP D'ÉTAT

The coup d'état, a recurring feature of Africa's political landscape, has left in its wake a litany of consequences that have reverberated across the continent. Beyond the immediate impact of overthrowing governments, coups have had profound and lasting effects on political stability, economic development, human rights, refugee crises, and much more. In this exploration, we delve into the multifaceted consequences of coups d'état in Africa, shedding light on the enduring challenges they pose to the region.

Political Instability

One of the most immediate and enduring consequences of coups d'état in Africa is political instability. While coups are often justified as attempts to restore order or rectify perceived injustices, they typically engender a period of turbulence and uncertainty. The abrupt removal of a government, even one deemed corrupt or ineffective, can lead to a power vacuum, intensifying political rivalries and power struggles.

Frequent coup attempts can create a cycle of instability, as new governments may face challenges in establishing legitimacy. The constant threat of coups can deter long-term planning and investment in democratic institutions, perpetuating a climate of political uncertainty.

Economic Problems

The economic ramifications of coups in Africa are profound. Economic stability is a critical component of development, and coups disrupt economic activities in several ways.

Firstly, coups often result in the suspension of economic activities, including trade, investment, and public services. International partners and investors may withdraw their support or adopt a cautious stance, fearing instability. This can hinder economic growth and development.

Secondly, coups can lead to economic mismanagement, as new regimes may prioritize consolidating power over sound economic policies. The misallocation of resources, corruption, and a lack of economic planning can exacerbate economic problems, leading to inflation, currency devaluation, and reduced economic opportunities.

Thirdly, the prolonged instability that often follows coups can discourage foreign direct investment (FDI) and deter international aid, which are essential sources of capital for many African nations. Reduced FDI and aid can constrain economic development efforts, exacerbating poverty and inequality.

Human Rights Abuses

Coups d'état in Africa have frequently been accompanied by egregious human rights abuses. Military regimes or coup leaders often resort to repression, censorship, and violence to maintain control. This can result in widespread violations of civil liberties and human rights.

Censorship of the media, suppression of political dissent, and curtailment of freedom of assembly are common tactics used to stifle opposition and maintain power. Arrests, extrajudicial killings, and torture may become commonplace, eroding the rule of law and undermining democratic values.

Women, children, and marginalized communities are often disproportionately affected by human rights abuses during and after coups. Sexual violence, forced displacement, and recruitment of child soldiers can be tragic consequences of political upheaval.

Refugee Crisis

Coups d'état in Africa can trigger refugee crises of considerable magnitude. The instability and violence that accompany coups often lead to mass displacement, both internally and across borders. People flee their homes to escape the chaos and violence, seeking refuge in neighboring countries or makeshift camps within their own nations.

This refugee crisis places immense strain on host countries' resources, infrastructure, and social services. It can also contribute to tensions between host communities and displaced populations, potentially fueling conflicts and exacerbating regional instability.

Furthermore, the displacement of skilled professionals and the disruption of education can have long-term consequences for human capital development and economic growth in affected regions.

Regional and International Implications

The consequences of coups in Africa extend beyond national borders. They can have significant regional and international implications.

Regionally, coups can destabilize neighboring countries through the spread of conflict, refugee flows, and economic disruptions. The regional organizations, such as the African Union (AU) and regional economic communities, often face the challenge of mediating conflicts and restoring stability in the aftermath of coups.

Internationally, coups can strain diplomatic relations. The international community, including Western governments, often condemns coup attempts and imposes sanctions on coup leaders and their supporters. These measures, while aimed at promoting democracy and human rights, can also have unintended consequences, such as exacerbating economic hardships for ordinary citizens.

Democracy and Governance

One of the most insidious consequences of coups in Africa is the erosion of democratic governance. The repeated interruption of democratic processes and the seizure of power by military or authoritarian regimes undermine the principles of democracy and the rule of law.

Democracy requires stable institutions, an independent judiciary, a free press, and respect for the electoral process. Coups disrupt these critical components of democracy, creating a climate where leaders may be more inclined to resort to unconstitutional means to attain or retain power.

Furthermore, coups often result in the sidelining of political opposition and civil society, weakening the checks and balances that are essential for a thriving democracy.

Long-Term Development Challenges

Perhaps one of the most enduring consequences of coups in Africa is the long-term developmental setbacks they create. The political instability, economic disruptions, human rights abuses, and displacement of skilled professionals hinder progress in key development indicators such as healthcare, education, and infrastructure.

Investment in long-term development projects becomes difficult in a climate of uncertainty. Poverty rates may rise, and access to essential services may decline, particularly in conflict-affected regions.

The loss of human capital, including professionals and skilled workers who may leave the country due to political instability or repression, also impedes development efforts. These challenges can hinder progress toward achieving the Sustainable Development Goals (SDGs) and improving the quality of life for African citizens.

Coups d'état in Africa are far-reaching and multifaceted. They encompass political instability, economic problems, human rights abuses, refugee crises, regional and international implications, erosion of democracy and governance, and long-term developmental challenges.

Addressing these consequences requires a concerted effort at both the national and international levels. African nations must prioritize democratic governance, conflict prevention, and the protection of human rights. The international community, including regional organizations and foreign governments, can play a crucial role in mediating conflicts, promoting peace, and supporting the restoration of democratic institutions in the aftermath of coups.

Ultimately, it is essential to break the cycle of coups in Africa to create a stable, prosperous, and democratic future for the continent and its people. This requires not only addressing the immediate consequences of coups but also addressing the root causes that give rise to them in the first place.

CHAPTER 4

FOREIGN INFLUENCE IN AFRICA

A number of military takeovers and coups have recently happened throughout Africa. Nine military takeovers or coups occurred throughout the globe between January 2021 and February 2022. Five of them Mali, Chad, Guinea, Sudan, and Burkina Faso were in Africa. The "successful" coups resulted in the continuation of the respective governments until the present. Since 2000, there have been more breakouts than ever before. Antonio Guterres, the secretary-general of the UN, bemoaned the situation and referred to it as an "epidemic of coup d'états."

Russia has played a key role in the military industry in Africa and has had a big impact on the wars there. Russia's network has grown to include nations including the Central African Republic, Chad, Niger, and Mali after starting in the Sudan. Its initial goal was to achieve financial gain via contracts with the military, but Moscow eventually added the political motive of enlarging its affiliated allies.

With over half of all weapons entering the African continent from Russia, it is now the region's top armaments supplier. Additionally, since 2016, Russian mercenaries have been discovered in more than 10 African nations. The Central African Republic, Sudan, and West Africa are among the countries where Wagner, a private Russian enterprise, conducts a variety of military operations. A business associated with the Wagner Group signed a 2021 contract for the deployment of around 1,000 mercenaries in Mali for 6 billion CFA francs ($9.74 million). Wagner has significantly increased its influence in the Central African Republic, and the government has nearly completely lost its ability to influence the company's actions. Additionally, Russia offers African nations information technology in the security field, such as internet misinformation operations and information control.

China has a significant presence in Africa in the economic and investment areas; between 2007 and 2020, Chinese development banks supplied $23 billion in finance for infrastructure projects in sub-Saharan Africa. This is more than what the World Bank has offered and more than twice the combined sum that the United States, Germany, Japan, and France have all loaned.

China has a history of refraining from meddling in the political affairs of other nations. This stands in stark contrast to Western nations, which provide aid in exchange for the acceptance of shared ideals like respect for democracy and human rights, and which take serious action after such ideals have been established. Over time, many African nations have learned to value China's noninterventionist approach. China's position is progressively shifting, however, as it has thoroughly ingrained itself in the economics and lifestyles of many African nations.

Based on its concept of "leaving African problems to Africa," China has always accepted the rulings of regional institutions like the Economic Community of West African States (ECOWAS). However, its current location has changed. China criticized the military coup in Guinea but said nothing about the one in Mali, although ECOWAS has recently adopted a tough stance against military coups. They seem to be forced to react differently in various situations as a result of the development of complicated interests.

China now has a far more substantial presence in Africa. Its strategy for Africa has altered in line with this, moving from an emphasis on infrastructure and building to partnership-oriented projects like enhancing commerce and connectivity. China designated Xue Bing, a prominent diplomat, as its first special representative for the "Horn of Africa," the eastern portion of Africa, in a statement in January 2022.

Other countries than only China and Russia are expanding their ties with Africa. Turkish President Recep Tayyip Erdogan, who aspires to restore the once-powerful "Ottoman Empire," has been to more than 30 African nations and shown a readiness to improve ties with the continent. Along with other Gulf nations, the United Arab Emirates (UAE) is enhancing its ties with Africa. At the UN Expert Group Meeting on Sudan, which was held in February 2022, UN experts discussed the extent to which the UAE financially supports the actions of Sudanese armed organizations.

Western nations, who have historically had a presence in Africa, are losing ground as other nations have increased their interest there. As a result of its inability to resolve lengthy wars, France, which has traditionally had significant sway over Francophone Africa, announced the departure of its armed forces from Mali in 2021.

The Russian engagement in Mali started soon after it was announced, and the Mali government dismissed the French ambassador in January 2022. In February 2022, the EU-AU summit was held, but African leaders expressed their "disappointment" since the help offered by European nations was less than anticipated, particularly when compared to promises from China and others. The United States and other Western nations have often suggested using sanctions against particular nations since they were formerly a powerful instrument for persuasion. However, it becomes less efficient since China, Russia, and other nations' increased involvement in Africa would open up loopholes.

The UN struggles to forge a consensus among the Security Council's P5 nations and is unable to play a significant role in intervening in crises. Although regional organizations like the African Union (AU) and ECOWAS do take action, such as suspending the membership of the problematic nations, the results are insufficient to alter the current circumstances.

It becomes difficult for any nation to overtly denounce strong power takeover by labeling them "coups," for fear of hurting ties with the countries in issue and losing diplomatic ground, given the number of players intimately engaged in Africa, some of whom assist coup attempts behind the scenes.

African nations were able to benefit greatly from aid by siding with either capitalism or socialism during the Cold War. Capitalism triumphed in the Cold War, and the democratic ideals of the West became the de facto norm to which no nation could object. While this was happening, the West lost interest in

Africa, leaving African nations to "fend for themselves."

The world has evolved. Many nations are now stepping up their links with Africa. They see enormous potential in Africa, where there are 100 cities with a population of over one million and room for future population expansion. The nations of Africa are no longer a remote continent from the rest of the globe. Instead, it is a chance for African nations to choose the partners they want. Influential African military and political figures now see coup attempts as a useful instrument they may use as needed.

CHAPTER 5

HOW COUP IN AFRICA IMPACTS CITIZENS AND FOREIGN RELATIONS

In the intricate tapestry of African politics, coups have often played a destabilizing role, sending shockwaves through nations and reverberating far beyond their borders. The aftermath of a coup d'état is not confined to the corridors of power; its consequences ripple through society, affecting ordinary citizens and reshaping diplomatic relationships with neighboring and foreign nations. Having witnessed the profound impact of coups in Africa, I delve into the intricate dynamics of how these abrupt changes of leadership can reshape lives and international ties.

Disruption of Daily Life

For the average citizen in an African nation experiencing a coup, life takes an abrupt turn. On the streets, there is an air of uncertainty and fear. Schools, businesses, and government offices may close, and curfews may be imposed. Access to essential services like healthcare and education can be severely disrupted, leaving families anxious about the well-being of their loved ones.

Public safety becomes a pressing concern. The sight of armed soldiers in the streets and the sound of gunfire or explosions can be a constant reminder of the volatility of the situation. Citizens often stay indoors, hoping to avoid the chaos and violence that can accompany a coup.

Economic Struggles

Coups d'état can have a devastating impact on the economy. Businesses may shutter their doors temporarily or even permanently, leading to job losses. Investors, both domestic and foreign, become wary of the political instability, and much-needed foreign direct investment (FDI) can dry up. Stock markets often plummet, and currency values can become highly volatile.

Inflation can surge as supply chains are disrupted, and uncertainty discourages investment. This, in turn, erodes the purchasing power of ordinary citizens, making basic necessities less affordable.

Human Rights Abuses

Perhaps one of the most distressing consequences of coups for citizens is the potential for human rights abuses. In the aftermath of a coup, there may be reports of arbitrary arrests, detention without trial, torture, and even extrajudicial killings. Citizens may be subjected to curtailed freedoms, such as restrictions on the media, curfews, and limits on freedom of assembly.

Minorities, political dissidents, and activists can face particularly severe repression. Women and children are often vulnerable to sexual violence, exploitation, and recruitment into armed groups.

Displacement and Refugee Crises

The displacement of people within the country and across borders is a direct consequence of coup-related violence. Families may be forced to flee their homes to escape the conflict, leading to a sudden influx of internally displaced persons (IDPs) in makeshift camps. The conditions in these camps are often dire, with limited access to clean water, food, and healthcare.

Neighboring countries often bear the brunt of refugee crises triggered by coups. Overwhelmed by the sudden influx of refugees, these nations may struggle to provide adequate shelter and assistance. This can strain relations between the coup-affected nation and its neighbors, potentially leading to tensions and conflicts over resources and security.

Diplomatic Relations with Neighbors

The diplomatic repercussions of coups are intricate and can have long-lasting effects on a nation's relationships with its neighbors. When a coup occurs, neighboring countries are often the first to react, and their responses can vary widely.

Some neighboring nations may condemn the coup and call for the restoration of constitutional order, while others may take a more cautious stance, opting for non-interference. Regional organizations, such as the African Union (AU), often play a pivotal role in mediating conflicts and restoring stability.

In some cases, neighboring countries may intervene militarily, either to support the ousted government or to protect their own security interests. These interventions can further escalate conflicts and strain relations between nations.

Foreign Relations

The impact of a coup in Africa on foreign relations extends beyond the immediate region. Foreign governments often react swiftly to coup attempts, issuing statements of condemnation and imposing sanctions on coup leaders and their supporters. These sanctions can have far-reaching economic consequences, affecting trade, investment, and international aid.

African nations facing coups may find themselves diplomatically isolated as foreign governments seek to uphold democratic norms and principles. The loss of international support can hinder efforts to address the root causes of the coup and restore stability.

Social Fragmentation

A coup d'état can deepen existing social divisions within a nation. Ethnic, religious, or regional fault lines may be exploited by coup leaders or factions, exacerbating tensions and potentially leading to communal violence. Social cohesion, a critical foundation for stability and development, can be eroded, making the process of post-coup reconciliation and nation-building all the more challenging.

Erosion of Trust in Institutions

Coup attempts can significantly erode trust in institutions and the political process. Citizens, already disillusioned by the coup, may lose faith in the ability of democratic institutions to protect their rights and promote their interests. This erosion of trust can have long-lasting effects, making it difficult to rebuild effective governance structures and civic engagement.

Brain Drain

In the wake of a coup, a "brain drain" phenomenon often occurs. Skilled professionals, intellectuals, and entrepreneurs may seek refuge in more stable countries, fearing for their safety or disillusioned by the political climate. The loss of human capital, expertise, and creativity can hamper economic development and impede post-coup recovery efforts.

Deteriorating Infrastructure

The upheaval caused by coups can result in the deterioration of critical infrastructure. Protests, violence, and looting can damage roads, utilities, and public facilities. The subsequent lack of maintenance and repair during periods of instability can further degrade infrastructure, hindering economic recovery and development.

Impact on Regional Security

A coup in one African nation can have repercussions on regional security. Armed groups and rebels may take advantage of the power vacuum created by the coup to escalate their activities, potentially destabilizing neighboring countries. Regional organizations and governments may be compelled to allocate resources to address these security threats, diverting attention and resources away from other critical development priorities.

Foreign Aid and Investment Reduction

In response to a coup, foreign aid and investment are often reduced or suspended. Donor nations and international financial institutions may withhold funding to express their disapproval of the coup, leaving the affected nation without critical resources for development projects, healthcare, and education.

Repercussions on Peacekeeping Missions

Many African nations contribute troops to international peacekeeping missions. A coup in a contributing country can disrupt these missions, impacting regional and international efforts to promote peace and security. Troop withdrawals or reallocations may be necessary, undermining peacekeeping operations and the stability of conflict-prone areas.

Erosion of National Sovereignty

Foreign intervention in response to a coup, even when well-intentioned, can lead to a perception of erosion of national sovereignty. This can create resentment and strain diplomatic relations with foreign nations, potentially hindering cooperation on various issues.

Cultural and Social Impacts

Coups can disrupt cultural and social life in profound ways. Arts, education, and cultural heritage may be neglected during periods of instability. Displacement and economic hardships can impact traditional ways of life, leading to the erosion of cultural practices and social fabric.

Diplomatic and Economic Isolation

Coup-affected nations often find themselves diplomatically and economically isolated. This isolation can hinder diplomatic negotiations, regional cooperation, and participation in international forums. Economically, it can limit trade opportunities and access to global markets, impeding the nation's economic growth potential.

The influence of a coup in Africa on its citizens and its relationships with foreign and neighboring communities is profound and far-reaching. For ordinary citizens, coups disrupt daily life, create economic hardships, and expose them to human rights abuses. The consequences of coups often lead to displacement and refugee crises, straining relations with neighboring nations.

On the international stage, coups trigger diplomatic responses that can range from condemnation to military intervention. The imposition of sanctions by foreign governments can further isolate coup-affected nations and impact their economic stability.

To mitigate these far-reaching consequences, it is imperative that African nations, regional organizations, and the international community work together to prevent coups, promote democratic governance, protect human rights, and address the root causes of political instability. Only through collective efforts can Africa hope to build a future of peace, stability, and prosperity for its citizens and its relationships with the global community.

CHAPTER 6

Solutions to the Coup d'État Problem in Africa

The recurring specter of coups d'état in Africa has had profound and far-reaching consequences, as explored in the previous section. To mitigate this persistent challenge and foster political stability, economic development, and democratic governance across the continent, comprehensive solutions are imperative. In this comprehensive examination, we delve into a range of strategies aimed at addressing the coup d'état problem in Africa, including strengthening democracy, improving governance, fighting corruption, promoting economic development, reforming the military, ensuring civilian control of the military, and providing better training and education for soldiers.

Strengthening Democracy

1. Democratic Education and Civic Engagement: Strengthening democracy begins with educating citizens about their

rights and responsibilities in a democratic society. Civic education programs can promote awareness of democratic principles, political participation, and the importance of peaceful transitions of power.

2. Free and Fair Elections: Ensuring that elections are free and fair is fundamental to democracy. African nations should invest in electoral commissions that are independent and transparent, enforce campaign finance regulations, and provide equal access to media for all political candidates.

3. Constitutional Reform: Comprehensive constitutional reform can help prevent power concentration and abuses. Reform efforts should focus on term limits, ensuring a fair balance of power between branches of government, and protecting the independence of the judiciary.

4. Inclusive Governance: Promoting inclusive governance is vital for political stability. Governments should actively involve diverse groups, including women, youth, and

minority populations, in decision-making processes. This inclusivity can foster social cohesion and reduce grievances.

5. Political Party Development: Building strong and accountable political parties is crucial for democracy. African nations can invest in capacity-building programs for political parties, promote internal democracy within parties, and establish mechanisms for campaign finance transparency.

Improving Governance

1. Anti-Corruption Measures: Corruption erodes trust in government and weakens institutions. African nations must implement and enforce robust anti-corruption measures, such as transparent procurement processes, whistleblower protections, and independent anti-corruption agencies.

2. Transparency and Accountability: Promoting transparency in government operations and fostering accountability mechanisms are

essential. Governments should publish budgets, expenditures, and contracts online, and create independent oversight bodies to monitor public spending.

3. Decentralization: Devolving power to local governments can enhance service delivery and responsiveness to citizens' needs. Decentralization efforts should be accompanied by capacity-building at the local level to ensure effective governance.

4. Rule of Law: Strengthening the rule of law is pivotal. African nations should invest in judicial independence, legal training, and access to justice for all citizens. A robust legal framework can safeguard individual rights and provide a forum for dispute resolution.

Fighting Corruption

1. Whistleblower Protection Enacting comprehensive whistleblower protection laws can encourage individuals to report

corruption without fear of retaliation. Such protections are essential for uncovering and addressing corrupt practices.

2. Asset Recovery: Recovering stolen assets from corrupt officials and their accomplices is crucial. African nations should collaborate with international organizations to trace and repatriate ill-gotten gains, deterring future corruption.

3. Public Awareness Campaigns: Raising public awareness about the corrosive effects of corruption can create societal pressure for change. Campaigns should educate citizens about the costs of corruption and the benefits of transparent governance.

4. Strengthening Oversight Bodies: Independent anti-corruption agencies and ombudsman offices play a critical role in uncovering corruption. These bodies should be adequately funded, staffed with skilled professionals, and granted the authority to investigate and prosecute corruption cases.

Promoting Economic Development

1. Diversification of Economies: Reducing economic dependence on a single commodity or sector can enhance economic resilience. Governments should implement policies that encourage diversification, support small and medium-sized enterprises (SMEs), and promote innovation.

2. Investment in Infrastructure: Adequate infrastructure, such as roads, energy, and telecommunications, is essential for economic growth. African nations should prioritize infrastructure development to attract investment and improve the business environment.

3. Access to Finance: Ensuring access to finance for entrepreneurs and SMEs can stimulate economic development. Governments can work with international financial institutions to create financing mechanisms and support financial inclusion.

4. Education and Skills Development: A well-educated and skilled workforce is critical for economic growth. African nations should invest in quality education and vocational training programs that align with the needs of the job market.

5. Regional Integration: Regional economic integration can create larger markets, facilitate trade, and attract investment. African countries should actively participate in regional economic communities and implement agreements that promote cross-border trade and cooperation.

Reforming the Military

1. Professionalization: African nations should prioritize the professionalization of their armed forces. This includes clear career paths, merit-based promotions, and a focus on military ethics and discipline.

2. Civilian Oversight: Establishing effective civilian oversight mechanisms over the

military is essential. Independent defense committees or parliamentary committees can provide civilian leaders with the necessary tools to monitor military activities and expenditures.

3. Human Rights Training: Military personnel should receive training on human rights and international humanitarian law. This training can reduce the likelihood of human rights abuses during conflicts or coup attempts.

4. Salaries and Benefits: Adequate compensation and benefits for military personnel can reduce the temptation to engage in coup plots due to financial pressures. Ensuring that soldiers are well-paid and have access to healthcare and housing can deter involvement in coups.

5. Disarmament and Demobilization Programs: For countries emerging from conflicts, disarmament and demobilization programs can help reintegrate former combatants into civilian life. These programs can reduce the pool of potential coup plotters.

Ensuring Civilian Control of the Military

1. Constitutional Safeguards: African nations should enshrine civilian control of the military in their constitutions, establishing clear legal frameworks that delineate the roles and responsibilities of civilian and military leaders.

2. Regular Elections: Ensuring regular, free, and fair elections is essential for maintaining civilian control. When leaders are elected by the people, it reinforces the legitimacy of the civilian government.

3. Respect for Chain of Command: The military should adhere to the principle of civilian supremacy, respecting the chain of command and the authority of elected civilian leaders.

4. Professionalization of Security Services: Security sector reform efforts should focus on the professionalization of police and other

security services, ensuring that they operate under civilian authority and adhere to human rights standards.

Providing Better Training and Education for Soldiers

1. Professional Military Education: Investment in professional military education institutions can enhance the skills and knowledge of military personnel. This education should include courses on leadership, ethics, and respect for civilian authority.

2. Human Rights Training: As mentioned earlier, human rights training is essential for soldiers to understand their responsibilities and the legal limits of their actions.

3. Leadership Development: Developing leadership skills among military officers can promote ethical behavior and a commitment to upholding democratic principles.

4. Mental Health Support: Soldiers often face traumatic experiences, especially during conflict situations. Providing mental health support and counseling services can help address the psychological challenges that some soldiers may face.

Addressing the coup d'état problem in Africa is a multifaceted endeavor that requires a holistic approach. Strengthening democracy, improving governance, fighting corruption, promoting economic development, reforming the military, ensuring civilian control of the military, and providing better training and education for soldiers are all interconnected strategies that can contribute to a more stable and prosperous Africa.

These solutions should be tailored to the unique circumstances of each African nation, recognizing that one-size-fits-all approaches may not be effective. Furthermore, international cooperation and support are essential to complement the efforts of African nations in addressing the root causes and consequences of coups.

By implementing these strategies and fostering a culture of democracy, transparency, and respect for human rights, African nations can reduce the likelihood of coups and create an environment conducive to political stability, economic growth, and the well-being of their citizens.